WALKING DEAD MAN

WALKING DEAD MAN

"What A Sleep Disorder
Can Do To You"!

"I was a walking dead man"!

F.D. Williams

To order additional copies of this book, contact:
Xlibris Corporation
1-888-795-4274
www.Xlibris.com
Orders@Xlibris.com
127840

Contents

Preface

This is a real-life story of what has happened to me. This is a story of my personal battle with a sleeping disorder.

This book may help save someone who has a sleeping disorder and does not know it.

Introduction

Have you ever asked, "What would I do in the time of trouble? When someone I love is rushed to the hospital? And when they tell me my loved ones may die?"

Chapter 1

Hardworking American

Just like other hardworking Americans, I worked *hard* to make a living for my family. My job was that of a tractor-trailer driver! I was a CDL class A driver. I operated a truck that had a gross weight of eighty thousand pounds. I worked up to seventy hours per week. I was required to work long days—up to fourteen hours per day. Working long hours required me to eat where I can—mostly fast foods like Burger King, Wendy's, or McDonald's. The long hours also had me drink a lot of soda pop. There is a lot of sugar in soft drinks, and over a period it will cause a person to have gain weight. Working long hours also made me become sleepy. When this happened, I would stop where I could. I ate food and drank sodas to stay awake. This may also cause weight gain due to the lack of sleep. And over a period of time, this can cause health problems.

This is a personal story of the things that have happened to me.

Working six days a week took up all my extra time. The only rest day I had was Sunday, and on that day, I only wanted to stay home and/ or visit other family members. I'd been so busy I had to pay someone to come and cut my grass. Working up to seventy hours was like working two jobs.

Just like many other Americans who work hard making a living for their families, taking no thought of what could happen to their health by working so many hours, not stopping to take a rest, not taking vacation time to enjoy life with their wife and children. I have had some people say, "Hard work has never killed anyone!" This book may change their mind.

Chapter 2

Warning Signs

While I was driving my truck, I began to notice many changes in my body. Just a few years earlier, I was able to drive long distances without getting tired or sleepy. In the past, I was able to drive for up to five hundred miles a day, only having to make a rest-area stop in order to use a restroom.

At that time, I felt like I could drive another five hundred miles without even being tired. At that time, I was feeling very good about my body, and at that time, I felt like I had no limitations or restrictions. Once I had received eight hours' sleep, I was good to go for another five hundred miles without any problems! It just seemed like I always had reserve energy—ready to go anytime. Whenever the boss needed extra work, I was always there and tried to be available whenever possible, always trying to be a good employee.

There were a lot of times I would work on holidays and weekends. I worked extra, picking up extra stops whenever or for a fellow employee who was out sick or on vacation. I always tried to help out whenever I could.

Then I began to notice *being very tired*. I saw that I was only driving about half as far as I was just a year or two before. My thoughts were that it's just old age and I would be just fine; however, everyone knows that when we get older, we just cannot work like we can when we were younger. My thought was I was just older. I was just going to have to deal with it—stopping more often, taking more breaks, doing what I could, and making changes in my driving style in order to deal with the changes of getting older.

As time went by, I gained thirty pounds in about six months. I just did not understand why I was gaining so much weight. I did not eat extra food. I was eating the same things; I just did not understand what it was.

My weight changed; fluid began building up in my body. My legs and feet were swollen. I could clearly see fluid building up in my body. My shoes did not fit properly, and I had to wear them loose or untied. I just could not figure out what was happening to my body. My feet and legs were bigger than they should be. There was something wrong! And I just didn't know what it was. I thought, *Something is wrong in my body*.

As time went by, I noticed that I began to gain a lot of weight. I also noticed that after about twenty miles, I became so sleepy that I could not hold my head up without falling asleep at the wheel.

That was not a very good thing to do while driving a tractor-trailer! I don't know if you believe in God, but my family and friends were praying for me. My daughter Rebecca had been praying for me a lot of times on the same day. I would have nearly wrecked my truck only to have a supernatural intervention from God.

God had protected me on many occasions. Several times I was on the verge of hitting a bridge or running off the road, but the Lord was there with his protecting hand. Prayer kept me from an accident in which I could have died.

Yes! My family prayed for me at the time when my health was failing, because they believed that God would hear and answer their prayers.

I would be at church, and while our pastor was preaching a Sunday message, I would fall asleep. My wife would try to wake me if she saw me falling asleep.

Our pastor and his wife knew that there was something wrong with me because it was very unusual for me to fall asleep during church. Our friends at church knew that there was something wrong with me. They would often say to me, "Are you feeling okay?" I would often say, "Yes! I'm not doing too badly today." But the whole time, they can see the change in me and the way that my body was reacting to my illness.

At work, there was little change in my job duties. I was still expected to perform all my responsibilities. No one was helping me whether I was able to do them or not. Many times I have prayed to the Lord. I would say, "Lord, there has to be an easier way to make a living. I just don't know how much longer I will be able to do these job duties that I have at the present time."

Due to all the weight gain and the fluid building up in my body, it became harder and harder to do my job. Some of my fellow employees saw my feet and leg swelling. Some of them said, "Your kidneys may not be working right." Others have said, "You may be having congestive heart failure." I would listen to what they had to say, and I would think to myself, *Could that be happening to me?*

As time went by, I began to wonder, Would I be okay? I could only see that my health was declining. Not knowing what I should do, and having to make a living for my family, I did that which my dad had told me to do as a man. He told me I had to be a good provider for my family.

I just had to keep on working so that they could have a place to live and food to eat. I was thinking only of my family and not thinking of myself. I was willing to die so that they might live, that they may have the things they needed in this life.

Their needs were food, clothing, a safe place to live, and protection. I wanted my wife to have a home. She told me many times, "I'd love to have a home—a nice home, a pond out back, and ducks flying into the pond." My wife said, "I love to see the ducks landing in the pond." All these things I was trying to do as a good provider for my home. The whole time I was doing these things, I knew something was wrong in my body, and I just did not know how to fix it.

I was able to buy my wife a nice home. And of course, there was a view of our neighbor's pond.

There, Tammy was able to see the ducks fly and land into the pond. I was doing everything I could to be a good husband—and that was providing for my family, giving my wife and children everything that they needed in order to have a good life—not knowing whether I would be there with them or whether I may pass away at any time due to health problems. As each day went by, my health declined to the point where I was just barely able to make it through the day. I began to develop an eye infection, and my wife told me that I needed to go to the doctor to see what was wrong.

So we made an appointment and went to see the doctor. And when I got to the doctor's office, the nurse began to take my oxygen level, and when she saw that my oxygen level was 74, she went out of the room and contacted the doctor. The doctor never went into the room. He just went to the phone and called for an ambulance. He told the emergency crew that he needed an ambulance—stat!

The next thing I knew, I was on my way to the hospital by ambulance.

At the hospital, they began to work with me. They placed me on oxygen. They did some blood work and placed me on four liters of oxygen. The nurses tried to take some more blood work. I saw that my blood had almost completely dried up in my veins. It was hard for the nurses to draw any blood out of my main artery. At that time, I knew it could kill me; I could possibly die.

In this next chapter, you'll see that I came close to death. Death is something that we all must face. But death is not the end. Life is a great journey! And the way that we live our lives, others will remember, including the things we've done for them.

Chapter 3

Facing Death

I would have died in twenty-four hours if I had not gone to the doctor!

The nurses returned to take my blood, and in doing so, they saw it was very difficult to extract any blood out of my veins.

The doctors were very concerned. By this time, the nurses had placed a full-oxygen mask over my head; my entire head was enclosed in the mask.

They placed me on steroids, testing blood every four hours to see if there was any improvement at all in the oxygen level in my blood.

Later that afternoon, the head nurse came and said to me, "We want you to try and go to sleep." But it was impossible! "We may need to resuscitate you in the event that you code. Do you want us to revive you?"

My wife and I began to talk things over about possibly having to resuscitate me. My wife and I agreed that if I had to be on the life-support machine to live, then they should just let me go ahead and die. After that, we told the nurse to only bring me back if I could live without being on a life-support machine. I told the head nurse, **"I am going to do what you have asked me! I am going to try to go to sleep. But you know that you have told me that it was possible that I may code.** So I am going to do what you have asked me to do and go to sleep."

So I simply went to sleep, and the next thing I knew, I was being rushed out of the ward to another ward in critical care. I think it was surprising to them that I awoke.

The emergency room doctor met us on the critical-care floor. To my surprise, the doctor told the head nurse, "He doesn't need to be here! He needs to go back where he was!" So the nurse turned me around and began taking me back to my former room. At that point, I knew that the emergency room doctor had seen something in the x-rays to know that God had moved for me, and I could tell in his voice that he knew that there was a supernatural power working for me and that I had made a turnaround.

After arriving back to my room under the nurses' care, I went back to sleep.

My wife was at my side the whole time. At that point, I told my wife, "We must live in the moment or day to day! We would have to take each day as it comes—dealing with issues as they arrive, living in the moment, trusting in the supernatural power of God and that God still has a plan for my life!"

By this time, my daughter who lived in Florida was on her way to be with our family. When she arrived, it was just good to see them again! I looked at all my family and told them, "I'm not sure if I will pull through or not!"

And I began to tell them of what had to be done the best that I could under the circumstances.

Our pastor and the members of our church were praying for us. Our pastor, Larry Myers, gave us a visit. It was good to see him again! We had other members from our local church visit us, and it was just good to see everyone again!

My wife never left my side; she was there to care for me and truly showed me how much she loved me.

They began running more tests and evaluated my progress every two to four hours to see if there was any improvement in my blood work and how much oxygen I had in my blood.

When you're sick like I was, there are a lot of unknown things you may not understand—things you just don't know, and a lot of questions. "What will tomorrow be like?" What we found out was, we had to live in the moment . . . day to day.

While I was in the hospital, it was to my surprise that God had people everywhere, and they were so concerned about my well-being. I recall a time when I was on my way to a test session. The nurse was humming a gospel song; it was so comforting to hear her humming that gospel song! There was just so much peace there in that elevator as the nurse was humming the gospel song. Oh! Oh! What a comfort it was. There was just something about the spirit of the Lord bringing peace in a time of trouble or in the time of sickness—there was just peace. When the Lord is with you, you just feel so relaxed, so peaceful.

People of the world may find it hard to understand the things of God, but those to whom God has revealed himself, they are those that have the understanding to know, to believe, and to receive the supernatural things of God!

> Jesus said unto him, if thou canst believe, all things are possible to him that believeth. (Mark 9:23)

> Again I say unto you, that if two of you shall agree on earth as touching anything that they shall ask, it shall be done for them of my father which is in heaven. (Matthew 18:19)

> For where two or three are gathered together in my name, there am I in the midst of them. (Matthew 18:20)

Jesus was faced with needing a touch of God in his life when he was praying in the garden of Gethsemane, and this was what Jesus prayed.

> And he went a little father, and fell on his face, and prayed, saying, O my father, if it were possible that this cup pass from me: nevertheless not as I will, but as thou wilt. (Matthew 26:39)

There comes a time in everyone's life that they need the supernatural touch from God. In the scripture above, you saw that Jesus himself prayed and asked God, "Let this cup pass from me." Jesus himself knew that man would need a supernatural touch and that only God could provide it.

There in that elevator, the humming of the gospel song was my comfort, my peace, my hope, and all my being I was trusting in the supernatural power of God.

It was so comforting to know, when all else fails and you have no hope, *there is hope!* And that hope is in Jesus Christ and what he did for man. Everything that Jesus went through in the garden of Gethsemane—that made a way for you and me that, in the time of trouble, we too could pray and ask for the Father's help. *That's what Jesus did!* He placed all his trust in God, and he was willing to face death so that you and I could live.

Then all of a sudden, the tension left me! I had comfort for a season of time; there was peace even in a time of trouble.

The Lord Jesus was there even in the middle of my sickness. I had been scheduled for a breathing test, and the nurse was taking me down for that particular test. After the test was over, they were waiting for someone to return me to my room. And while I was waiting, I was able to share the message of Jesus Christ and the things of God to all those who were running tests on me. Even in the hospital, I had a joyous time sharing about Jesus and my love for him!

There were many other times that the nursing staff shared their faith with me, comforting me even in the time of my sickness. God always has someone who will pray for you in the time of your sickness . . . or in the time of trouble.

We have to live in the moment, making changes and taking things hour by hour and day to day.

After several days of medical care, I still did not know how long I would be in the hospital, or if I would live! My wife and I were living in the moment and day by day and facing things as they came by, adapting to the situation and making decisions as soon as we faced it, finding a solution for the problem.

Sometimes we need more than medical help; we need supernatural help. You will find out more in the next chapter about supernatural help.

Chapter 4

Supernatural Help

Some people may not understand supernatural help, and others will believe in supernatural help. This is a story of my supernatural help and what God did for me through others who were praying for me.

After many days of seeing that my health was about the same, I was now receiving plenty of oxygen. My body seemed to be adjusting well. I didn't seem to be as tired as I had been in the past, and my wife and I were still living in the moment and day to day.

Everyone was praying for me, and my in-laws were also in prayer for me. The Parker family went to visit me in the hospital. Chris's mom, Debbie, had been led by the Lord to start working on a large prayer shawl. She didn't know whom it was for; she had been preparing this prayer shawl for almost two years.

In preparing this prayer shawl, Chris's mom had made some trips out to the state of New Mexico. New Mexico, USA, was a special place to the Parker family as well as to our family.

Chris married Jennifer, my daughter, and several years earlier, we had made a missionary journey to the state of New Mexico and ministered to the Navajo Indians.

We set up a gospel tent and ministered to the Navajo Indians on their reservation. We told the Navajo people that God had a plan for their lives and there was a better way to live.

We brought the Navajos clothing, food, toys for the children, and the good news that Jesus was the answer to all the problems that they had to face. It was a very special time in my life as well as in their families' lives. The Indians were a very special people to me as well as to my daughter.

After the Navajo revival, my daughter Jennifer, Chris, and youth ministers Tim and Pam Shepherd were led by the Lord to move to the state of New Mexico and start a church and began ministering to the Navajo Indians, and they ministered out there for many years.

After ministering to the Navajos in New Mexico, they moved to the state of Florida. Our family has a Cherokee Indian heritage; Indians are special people to us.

The Parker family went to the hospital with a prayer shawl. My wife, my daughter, and my wonderful church sister, Linda Swim—they had all been praying over the prayer shawl, not knowing whom it was for, not knowing that it would be used for someone they knew.

When the Parker family brought in the prayer shawl, my wife then realized what it was (the prayer shawl that they had been praying over). They then placed the prayer shawl over me, and everyone began praying, and at that time, I literally felt my insides just like I can sense my whole intestinal system beginning to operate again, just like starting an engine! I heard the noise like that of a motor. I could feel my whole digestive system beginning to operate. Before me, as though I can see a vision, I saw bones in the desert. I saw a coyote snarling and a big bird flying. My thought was that it looked like a buzzard. As this big bird flew over my head, as it passed over me, I heard the cry of an eagle; and my thought was that it was an eagle. At that time, I realized that I was seeing a vision and that the supernatural power of God was moving for me.

(Picture on the next page is the prayer shawl that was made for me.)

Prayer Shawl

Surely he shall deliver thee from the snare of the fowler, and from the noisome pestilence. (Psalm 91:3)

He shall cover thee with his feathers, and under his wings shall thou trust: his true shield and Buckle. (Psalm 91:4)

All this was in just a moment of time. Ancestors before me had visions; I too had a vision quest. Chris's mom said to me at that time that the Lord was not through with me yet; there was still work here that I had to do.

My health improved some day by day. Little by little, I began to feel better. The doctors and the nurses that were treating me were keeping up with my progress. After about six days, they began to tell me that I may be able to go home. That sure was good news for me and my wife. She had been so faithful, staying with me day and night, taking care of me, showing me her love. I truly do appreciate everything that she has done for me.

After the ninth day, I finally got to leave the hospital. We finally made it home. My recovery would be a long process. There would be a big change in our income. I would not be able to return to work for a long period of time. But it was good to be home again! We would have to make some big changes to my sleeping area.

When I arrived home, we had to prepare a sleeping area. It was hard for me to lie down in a normal bed. I had to sleep in an upright position or in a reclined position. The doctors diagnosed me with sleep apnea. They gave me a loaner sleep apnea machine; I was to use it until they could do a sleep study.

A sleep study is needed to determine if there is a blockage to the airway or if the airway is closing. It also determines if you quit breathing. It allows the doctors to see if oxygen is needed to keep the oxygen level up in the blood. Good oxygen levels are needed to keep the brain working properly. It also helps the body to regenerate itself while at sleep. The body also removes poisons from the blood. The body cleanses itself while sleeping and at rest. Sleep is a very important part of good health.

I was told by my nursing staff that I needed a minimum of four hours of continuous sleep using my sleep apnea machine. Or I would be right back in the hospital if I had less than four hours of sleep each night on the sleep apnea machine. But we truly need six to eight hours of sleep for our body to get the rest that it needs.

Tammy wanted to see ducks flying over the pond. Here it is! The view is from our back deck. The fence is our property line.

Tammy loves to see the ducks in the pond!

Chapter 5

My Sleep Studies

After I got home, I found myself having to sleep in the recliner for many nights.

I was on three liters of oxygen using a portable oxygen bottle. I had to roll it around with me each day while away from home.

I was on an oxygen generator while at home. I had been using it with my sleep apnea machine continuously, and after several months, we made an appointment to do a sleep study. During the sleep study, the nurse told me she wanted to see how I would do in a normal sleep. And after that, she had the test results. She, at that time, placed me on the sleep apnea machine; she then began to monitor the tests and, if she needed to, added oxygen. After she completed that test, she woke me from sleep.

I was hooked up to a machine that monitored my heart rate and oxygen level. This machine could tell the doctors and nurses if my heart quit beating and if the air passages were closing. It also monitored the pulse rate.

After the test was over, the nurse woke me from sleep. She said that they would give the report to the doctors, and he would be able to tell me what the results were.

Finally, all the tests were over. At that time, we began to make an appointment to see what the doctor found out about the sleep study tests. My wife and I wanted to hear what the results were. So he made an appointment to see what the sleep apnea test results were.

Chapter 6

Test Results

The test results were very surprising!

The day at the doctor's office finally came.

It finally came. I saw my doctor for the first time. The day of the test results was here; finally, I would be able to see what they were.

The doctor looked at my test results and told me I had quit breathing over one hundred times in a minute. I could have died at any moment while sleeping!

I could have left this world, not ever seeing my family again, or them never seeing me again! In this life, it is something to face death, never knowing when it may come! Only the grace of God spared my life, and for this, I'm so thankful—that God answered prayers and that he had people who loved me and prayed for me that I might live and not die. For this, I thank God—that he spared my life. And I wanted to tell others that he is a good god and that he answers prayers.

The Bible says, "All things are possible to him that believes." This is found in Mark 9:23. The prayer shawl was a point of contact. On this prayer shawl were Psalm 91:3, "Surely he shall deliver the from the snare of the Fowler, and from a noisome pestilence," and Psalm 91:4, "He shall cover thee with his feathers, and under his wings shalt thou trust: His truth shall be thy shield and buckler."

I don't know if Debbie Parker knew that my favorite psalm was Psalm 91 or not. But a few years earlier, I had fixed a summertime outdoor shirt, and embroidered on the back of it was Psalm 91. I had wanted everyone to know that I believed in God and put my trust in him. It was my way of witnessing to others who do not know God.

So I wore the Psalm 91 shirt to be a witness to others. I did not know that, in my future, Psalm 91:3 and Psalm 91:4 would minister to me in my life.

I thank God for the power of his Word!

Chapter 7

Doctor's Diagnosis

The doctors diagnosed me with sleep apnea. They told me that sleep apnea happens when the airway tries to close and doesn't stay open while a person is sleeping. And when this airway closes, a person stops breathing, and the body's defense mechanism is to try to wake up that individual. It would say, "It's time to wake up! I'm not breathing!"

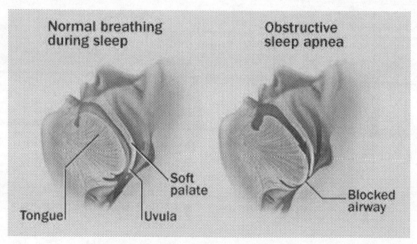

Carilion Sleep Center

<<Picture on right is a blocked airway. Picture on the left is a nonblocked airway.>>

All of my tests were done by the Carilion Sleep Center and my Carilion physicians. Information in this book came from my personal treatments on what I've been told about by my personal sleep apnea condition.

Pictures like the one on the previous page can be seen or viewed at any sleep center in your local community or in any websites or clinics for the treatment of sleep apnea. You may visit your local hospital or clinic for more information pertaining to sleep apnea and its treatments.

My doctor prescribed me with a sleep apnea machine to be used to keep my airway open while I am sleeping. At night, air pressure from the machine prevents my airway from closing; therefore, my airway continues to stay open, and I can have a normal night of sleep. My body is able to cleanse itself and get the proper rest it needs, and my lungs and my brain will receive the proper amount of oxygen so that the body can work properly.

Doctors told me that a lot of my overweight problems came from my body not getting the proper amount of rest that it needed because I was working long hours and had very little sleep. This did not allow my body to get the minimum amount of sleep that is required for it to regenerate itself.

So with that information and what they have told me, I knew then that my job was killing me because I was not receiving the proper amount of rest. Therefore, the hard work, in my case, was killing me. The doctors told me that the body needed a minimum of four hours of continuous sleep. *Four hours of continuous sleep* at the very minimum, or my body would start having the problems that I was having. My oxygen level would be restricted; my body would not be able to cleanse itself. This would cause weight gain due to the fact that I'll have to eat to stay awake and that my body would not cleanse itself or digest food properly due to the lack of sleep and not having proper amount of oxygen.

Everyone should get six to eight hours, preferably eight hours, of sleep each night to prevent problems from developing or having a sleep disorder.

Doctors said to try to stop any weight gain and that weight gain can cause a restriction to the air passage. And losing weight would be a big help in improving my sleep apnea condition. Maintaining a proper weight is a big help when battling a sleeping disorder.

For anyone who has a sleeping disorder, the doctors recommend losing weight and maintaining your weight to improve sleep apnea conditions.

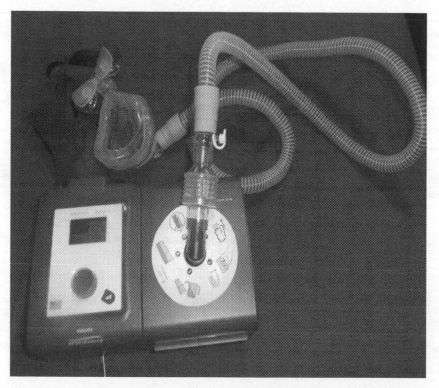

This is a picture of my sleep apnea machine.

On the picture of my sleep apnea machine, notice the hose and the mask. The mask covers my nose and my mouth, and air comes from the machine through the hose and keeps my airway open.

I have to wear this each night while I'm sleeping so that my airway will remain open and that I would not stop breathing while I was sleeping.

When a person's airway closes, the body can't receive the proper amount of oxygen. And when oxygen is restricted, the body cannot operate properly.

Chapter 8

A Very Trying Time

Like with any sickness, there is a time of recovery or a time in which your health is improving.

After my visit with the doctor, it wasn't fun pulling an oxygen bottle around everywhere I went. Portable oxygen was very expensive; by this time, my health insurance from a former employer was running out, and I had lost my salary.

I only had a limited number of sick days. Once I used my vacation time and my sick days, I will not receive any more money from my employer.

My employer placed me on sick leave. My employer would hold my job for six months. After that, I would simply be replaced. I had been employed there for almost fifteen years. There seemed to be no short-term disability plan, nor was there any long-term disability plan.

My wife and I were living on her salary and the kindness of our family members, our local church family, and our wonderful friends who sacrificed and gave out of their hearts in order for us to meet our needs. I can recall a time when my house note was due and I had no way of making my payment. My wife went to the mailbox, and there was a letter in there addressed to me. And in that letter was a check that met all my needs for my house note that month.

After seeing the check, I just sat there and gave thanks to the Lord with tears streaming down my face! **"Thank you, Lord,** for laying it on people's hearts to help us in the time of our need."

A wonderful church lady whose name is Linda Swim and her daughter, Cathy, and her husband, Brian, have gone out of their way and treated us as if we were one of their own family.

Sister Linda would take us to church so we didn't have to buy gas, helping us any way she could in order to see our needs met. She has been more than a friend; she literally has become part of our family! And we truly love her very much.

Our family thanks her for all her kindness and generosity. She has truly shown the love of God by helping us in the time of our need.

Our local church family: special thanks to our pastor, Larry, and Wanda Myers of the Cool Springs Pentecostal Holiness Church. They also have helped us in the time of our need, and we want to say thank you to everyone in our church family.

Like with any sickness, there are trying times. You always wonder, *How will I pay my bills? Where will I get the money I need?*

There are just some things that are out of our control, and we have to rely on a supernatural intervention in order to have what we need in this life. We simply have to trust and rely on a supernatural power; that's why I have faith in God! Because I know—there is more to life than living in the natural man.

We have to put our faith and our confidence in someone who can help us in the time of our need. That's what I, as well as my family, have found—that we must trust in God's supernatural power. And we have put our trust in the supernatural power of God and his son, in whom God created the world through his spoken word, who is Jesus Christ—our savior, our redeemer, our way-maker, and our soon-coming king. There's one thing I have found out—we cannot make it on our own! We truly need God in our life. There is more than just dying and going to the grave. I look at the trees, I look at the grass, I look at the sky, and I say, "Look at this creation!" The work of a supernatural god, who made everything I see, and I know that there's more than living in the natural man.

In this natural man, there is a spiritual man, and that spiritual man will live forever. See, when you're sick, you simply do not want to die! So our family has decided to believe and to trust in a supernatural god. And the only god that I know of that has risen from the dead, that living god is Jesus Christ. He is the only god who has promised to return for his people. And we have chosen to follow him. It is in this faith that I began to believe in before and during my sickness to help me when doctors can't help me.

There is a picture of an oxygen bottle, on the next page, that I had to pull around everywhere I went when I was not home. And believe me, it was not a fun thing to do! My goal was to become oxygen-free and to believe the Lord for an improvement in my condition.

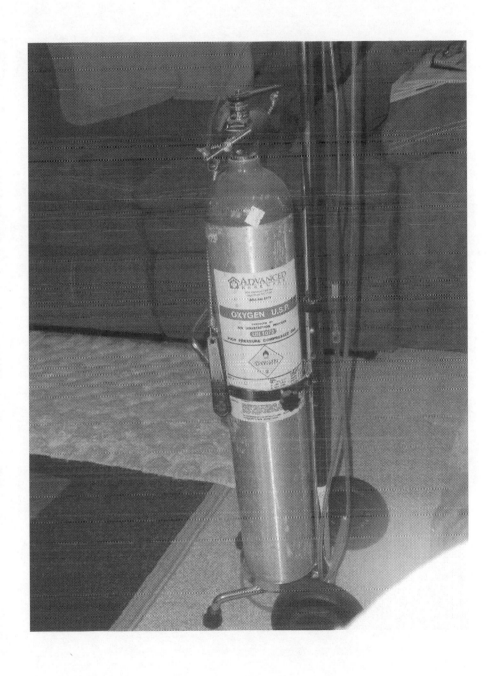

Freedom from the oxygen bottle is on the way.

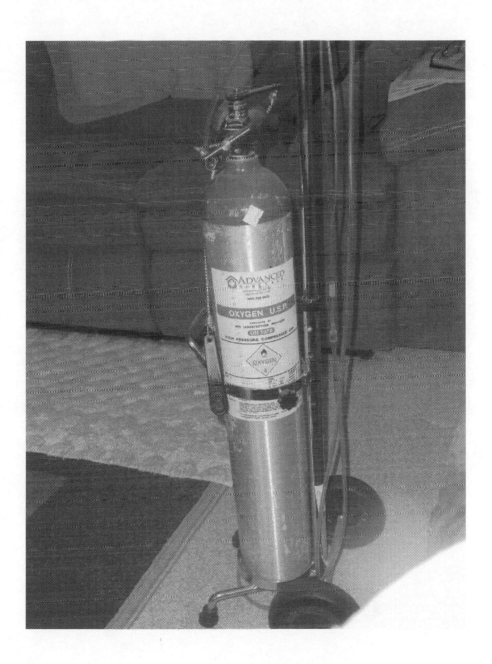

Every time I left home, I had to make room for the oxygen bottle! After several weeks of not being able to go to church, finally did so. I would take the oxygen bottle with me and use the oxygen until we got to the church. And at that point, I would tell my wife, "I am not wearing this inside the house of God!" I believe that started a miracle for me. Every time that I would go to church, when I got there, I would leave the oxygen bottle in the car, go inside for worship service, return to the car, and start wearing the oxygen home. And when I got home, I started using my home-oxygen concentrator. But when it came to church time, I wanted to be free of the oxygen bottle. God honored my faith! And over a period of several months, I had improved enough to come completely be off the oxygen during the day. Thank God! I didn't have to use it anymore.

You may have physical challenges, you may have financial challenges, you may even have a lack of food; but there's one thing for sure—from my heart, I want to tell you to put your trust in God and in his son, Jesus Christ. In doing so, you will see the hand of God move for you in the time of your need.

Chapter 9

Our First Grandson

And Still a Trying Time!

The time came for my daughter, Jennifer, and her husband, Chris to leave the hospital. Both would return to their home in Florida. They had witnessed that my health was improving. Both of them had to return to Florida because their employers were expecting them to return to work. In the meanwhile, the days and the weeks passed by. My wife and I were dealing with my health and making adjustments day to day.

One day, the thought came to me that I needed to pray for my oldest daughter, Jennifer, that God would open her womb and that she would conceive a child.

I could sense the spirit of the Lord telling me to pray

We read in Genesis 29:31-35:

> And when the Lord saw that Leah was hated, he opened her womb: but Rachel was barren.

And Leah conceived and bare a son, and she called his name Ruben: for she said, surely the Lord hath looked upon my affliction; now therefore my husband will love me.

And she conceived again, and Bare a son; and said, because the Lord hath heard that I was hated, he therefore had given me this son also: and she called his name Simeon.

And she conceived again, and bare a son; and said, Now this time will my husband be joined unto me, because I have born him three sons: therefore was his name called Levi.

And she conceived again, and bare a son: and she said, now will I praise the Lord: therefore she called his name Judah: and left bearing.

The scriptures are clear that God is the one who opens the woman's womb for her to conceive a child. And I truly wanted to obey the Lord and to his spirit. So I picked up the phone and dialed Jennifer's phone number, but she didn't answer the phone. All I got was the voice mail, so I left a message. I began to tell her over the phone that I believed that the Lord was going to open her womb, that she would be able to conceive a child. So I just prayed for her over the phone that these things would happen. I don't remember how long it was. It may have been a few hours or a day. I really don't know, and I don't remember.

But she returned my call and said to me, "It's a funny thing that you would call and pray for me to conceive a child, for I have found out that I am expecting a child!" And we were very thankful and very happy that she was expecting our first grandchild. She conceived a child. There was no doubt in my mind that while they were there with me at the hospital, God had given my daughter a favor. While my daughter's heart was toward me, asking God for my healing, my god had given her favor! God had opened her womb as he did for Leah. It was a happy time for everyone. They had seen God move for me and spare my life! And now Jennifer and Chris were being blessed by the Lord to conceive their first child.

Several months went by, and Jennifer began to have some problems with swelling in her feet and legs, and the doctors were watching her progress to determine what was going on in her body, that she was having water retention during her pregnancy. A lot of women do gain water weight while they are expecting, but it can cause health problems.

There is a health problem called preeclampsia, which develops while a woman is expecting a child. Doctors were monitoring her and her condition. In the meantime, my wife, Tammy, and I were still dealing with my health issues. She was helping me keep my doctor's appointments, helping me to fill out my paperwork; by this time, the doctors had determined that I would not be returning to work because of all my health complications.

Our family doctor at that time was Dr. Linick. She had told me that with all that I had been through with my health problems, needed to fill out my disability papers. And with all the problems that I had while driving a truck, it would be a good thing not to return to work or to those job duties because those had contributed to all my health problems. My doctor told me that the long hours of driving and no sleep had placed me in sleep deprivation (lack of sleep that could not be made up) and that the truck-driving job almost cost me my life and that it was time for me just to simply retire and enjoy what life I had remaining, spending time with my family and friends.

So my wife and I started filling out the proper paperwork. As time went on, Jennifer had now been over six months in her pregnancy. She would call from time to time and talk with her mother to see if her mother had any problems when she was carrying her or if she had any weight gain due to water retention. Jennifer asked her mother this question: "Mom, did your feet swell?" Her mother's reply was, "Yes, some." As time went by, we became more concerned with Jennifer's health. I think it was around March 2011 when we finally got to see them. At that time, we could tell that her feet and legs were swelling and that she was very uncomfortable. While sitting, she would try to keep her feet elevated in order to help out with the swelling. We started thinking that it will not be too much longer and it would all be over because she was nearing her seventh month of pregnancy.

Even when you're going through a sickness in your life, there are other people who are dealing with sicknesses in their lives. We don't live in a perfect world! Every family will have to deal with sicknesses, deaths, and financial hardships. All these things are a part of life. Jennifer was on her thirty-third week of pregnancy, and we received a phone call from Chris. To the best of my memory, Chris informed us that they were going to have to do an emergency C-section on Jennifer, that she was experiencing difficulty and having pregnancy complications. The doctor said she had preeclampsia and they would have to take the baby by C-section. So we grabbed our clothing, loaded up the truck, and headed for Florida to be in support of Jennifer during her time of illness.

Chris's mom, Debbie Parker, asked if she could go with us, and we said, "Sure!"

On the way down there, I really didn't feel comfortable and was concerned about Jennifer's surgery. Numerous times I prayed for Jennifer while driving to Florida. I asked the Lord to intervene, to protect her and the baby. Jennifer is a wonderful gospel singer, and I reminded the Lord that she still had songs to sing for his glory. I believed that he had allowed her to conceive and that he had a plan for the baby's life.

It was around thirteen hours' drive; it was the longest drive that I had made since my illness. I had been a truck driver for a long time, and I had some long days. I was just trusting in the Lord that I would be able to make that long journey without having any difficulties in my health. We had to take along with us a portable oxygen generator that I could use so that I could have the proper amount of oxygen while sleeping at night.

<<Picture of an oxygen generator>>

Chris called later that afternoon and said that the baby was okay and they had put him in an incubator. But Jennifer was still having some problems, and they were not sure about her yet. She was having blood pressure problems, and they were trying to regulate her blood pressure. The only thing we could do at that time was just pray.

We finally got to the hospital, and when we got there, Jennifer was awake and was able to talk with us. It was so good to see that she was doing so much better. By this time, everyone was wanting to see the baby. Jennifer and Chris gave the baby the name Landon Christopher Parker, and we were going to get to see him for the first time.

I got to go back and see him, and I saw that they had placed him in an incubator, and he had to use an oxygen mask just like I had, so I can relate to the care that he was needing. We could reach in and touch his hand. So I reached in and touched his little hand, and Landon opened his hand and placed his hand around my finger. At that time, the tears just ran down my face, and I began to pray for Landon, thanking God for him, asking the Lord to touch him in his body. This was truly a blessing even though he was going through an illness just like I was. We all knew that there was hope. In Jesus, there is always hope, and we were all trusting in him!

Landon in Winnie Palmer Hospital

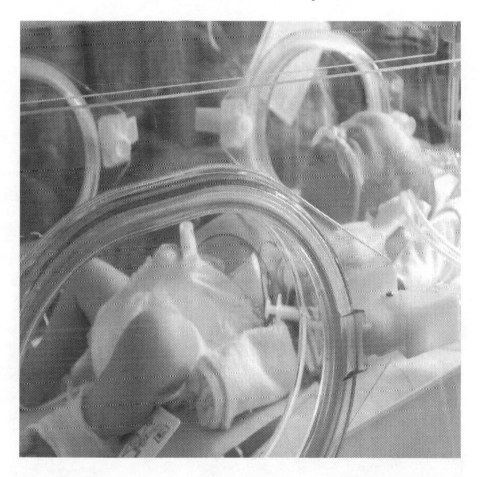

Winnie Palmer Hospital

Orlando, Florida

Landon continued to stay in the hospital for approximately four weeks after our visit. He was kept in an incubator, and the doctors monitored his vital signs. The doctors had told Jennifer and Chris that he would have to remain in the hospital until his lungs were fully developed and he was able to breathe on his own and keep the oxygen level up in his blood. At that time, he would be permitted to go home.

That simply was just good news for our whole family! In the meantime, I wanted to start reducing my dependency on an oxygen tank at night while using the BiPAP machine. So I told my wife that I wanted to start reducing the amount of oxygen that I was using at night and gradually wean myself off the use of oxygen. Of course, she was concerned that I might come off the oxygen too quickly. I told her that I believed that my body was trying to make an adjustment and that right now my oxygen level was really high, and I felt that I could reduce the oxygen level and still have a good level of oxygen in my blood and then my body could make the adjustment that it needed. At that time, we decided to give it a try and began to wean myself off the use of oxygen. I was, at that time, using approximately three liters of oxygen. I began to reduce my oxygen level by one-half liter.

My body would always let me know whether I was getting enough oxygen or not. I would always get a feeling of discomfort if my body was not receiving enough oxygen.

While spending time with Landon, it gave me the desire to try to remove my dependency on oxygen or having to use oxygen at night. It took my body a couple of nights to make adjustments, and at that time, I saw that my body was making the proper adjustments and that my oxygen level was improving even with the reduction of one-half liter at a time.

Landon's health was improving. Jennifer, his mom, was improving also. Everything was going well, so we decided that we needed to return to Virginia so that my wife could return to work and I could continue trying to improve in my health.

Upon arriving in Virginia, we all needed a good rest. We stayed in contact with the family in Florida and continued to monitor their progress and how they were improving in their health. And in the meantime, I continued to work on reducing the amount of oxygen that I needed at night while on the sleep apnea machine. After a few weeks, I began to see that my body was telling me that I could still make an adjustment on my oxygen level, so I continued to reduce the amount of oxygen by one-half liter. I was now down to two liters of oxygen at night while using the sleep apnea machine.

I thought it would be best at this time to stay on this reduction rate for at least four months in order to allow my body to adjust to the new amount of oxygen I was receiving from the sleep apnea machine.

Adjustment to the amount of oxygen is made using the knob at the top right corner.

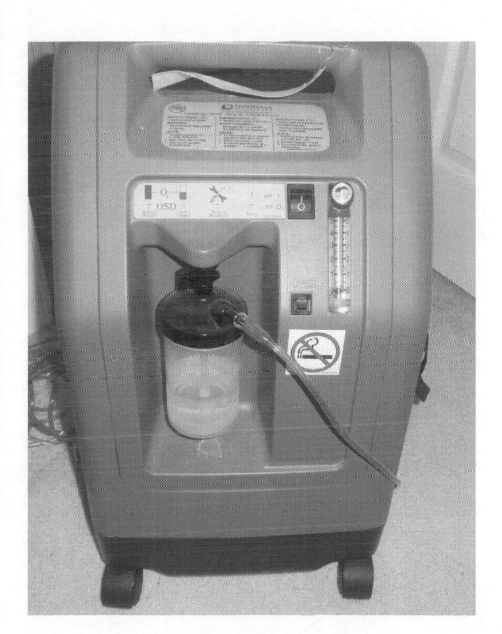

Chapter 10

Finances Devastated

In dealing with a long-term illness, you find yourself having to make adjustments in the family income, still hoping that you would have the finances needed to pay all your bills. I had been the primary breadwinner for our family, and now I had to make major adjustments to the income. I had completely lost my job, and at this point, I had no financial income and will not have any financial income as we had heard that I had to be off work for six months prior to receiving any disability and that I will not be receiving any back pay for the six months that I had not worked.

My employer had told me that I had no short-term disability or long-term disability. The only help that we had was family members, our church family, and special friends. We soon found out that none of our creditors were willing to work with us in any manner whatsoever. No one wanted to give us an extension. No one offered to help us. All the creditors expected their money regardless of the circumstance and regardless of what my family was facing at the time.

My family and I had made every effort to pay our bills on time. I had an outstanding credit rating. I could borrow up to $45,000 on my signature. I had borrowed money to buy our new home with my signature alone and without a down payment. Even the closing cost was included with my mortgage, and I had no out-of-pocket expense whatsoever. But still, at this time, no one wanted to take into consideration that my sickness prevented me from being able to pay my bills on time.

My wife and I had always said that we would live in the moment and day to day. We simply had no other choice but to go seek legal advice and obtain a lawyer. The creditors were very dogmatic, wanting their money now, so we had no other choice but to seek help from an attorney and the laws of the land. My salary at the time of my sickness was in excess of $50,000 a year, and I had made as much as around $62,000 a year.

Again, if you remember I said early on that I was a professional CDL driver and worked up to approximately seventy hours a week. I had worked long hours, six days a week. And the reward I got from paying my bills on time was a collection notice in the mail!

I told my wife that we had no other choice but to seek advice from the attorney and to take action immediately! I simply was not going to put up with any more harassment from the creditors. We had worked hard all our lives, and we had a mobile home on a land that was a little over an acre and was completely paid for. We had a clear deed to the property and to the home. Our lawyers and the courts told us that we would have to give up the home and the land that was paid for and that it was going to have to be sold and the money would have go to the creditors. So we were faced with losing everything that we had ever worked for and having to start over.

Our new home that we had just bought, the courts asked us about that also. But the good thing was, we owed more money on the home than the home was worth, and we would be able to stay in the home as long as we were able to make the payments.

At the time of the writing of this book, we are still in our new home, and thanks to the Lord, we have been able to make the payments.

It's hard for any family to think about losing $50,000 a year without any means of making up for that income.

The courts had told us that we could only have $10,000 in assets, which included cars, furniture, and personal belongings. Anything over that would have to be given to the courts. Those items would be sold, and the monies received would be given to the creditors in order to pay for the debt.

My wife was the only one working at that time, and the courts told my wife that the money that the court had requested for repayment to the creditors would have to be taken out of her check until all the creditors were satisfied.

We were not only dealing with a major sickness, but we were also dealing with financial devastation.

It is a trying time when the family loses an income and has no way to make up for it. The only thing that we can hope for and have faith in is God.

Looking back over my life, I see where I had always tried to make a living by my own ability (on what I could do in my ability), not in what

God can do through his ability. I have learned through this experience that we must trust in God and his ability, trusting him that our every need would be met.

> And Jesus answering say unto them, have faith in God. (Mark 11:22)

> For verily I said to you that whosoever shall say unto this mountain, are (be) thou removed, and be thou cast into the sea: and shall not doubt in his heart, but shall believe that those things which he saith shall come to pass; he shall have whatsoever he saith. (Mark 11:23)

> Therefore I say unto you, what things so ever you desire, when ye pray, believe that ye receive them, and ye shall have them. (Mark 11:24)

During a period of financial devastation, one must find and have hope in something that is beyond his personal control, and that source is supernatural help. In the scriptures on the previous page, we find the source of help—that source of help is faith in a supernatural god moving a financial mountain that attacks the lives of common (everyday) people everywhere. When we have done everything possible to obtain the essentials of everyday life and fallen short, we must put our trust in the supernatural provision of God.

> Behold the fowls' of the air: for they sow not, neither do they reap, nor gather into barns; yet your heavenly father feed'eth them. Are you not much better than they? (Matthew 6:26)

My wife and I have chosen to live in the moment and day to day. And if someone you know is going through a struggle at this time in their life, my prayer is that you put your confidence, trust, and faith in the supernatural power of God and in his supernatural word.

Chapter 11

Entering into a New Season of Life

Many changes were taking place in our lives. My wife and I had been adapting to every situation. There were many things that we were going to have to continue to deal with.

I can recall a time when I had asked my wife about how she had felt concerning whether or not I would be receiving my disability insurance. I can recall asking her, "Do you think that I will qualify to receive my disability payments?" I remember asking her on a couple of occasions about the situation because I was concerned.

Then suddenly, one day in particular, I recall asking her the same question. And on this day, she gave me a quick response, and her immediate reply was "Yes! You're going to receive your disability insurance."

That day, the spirit of the Lord had given her the answer to my question. I had been praying about it, but I had not received any confirmation from the Lord at this time whether I would receive it or not. And I wanted to ask my wife the question to see if the Lord had given her the answer to the question, and on that day, God gave her the answer to the question!

We finally heard about my disability insurance, and we found out that all the doctors as well as the disability agents had agreed that I was entitled to my disability and that I would begin to receive payments soon after my six months of unemployment. This was a very trying time for me and my wife. I had seen so many people that had been turned down, and I didn't know whether I would be able to qualify.

I know that I am truly entering into my fall season of life. If we look at the natural seasons, we have spring, summer, fall, and winter. Let us take a look at life in general. A newborn baby, with his/her mother—it is a new life! And we can say that it is spring because of the newness of life. And then we can look at the young adult years and say that it is summer. When we reach the age of around forty and into our fifties, we can say that we are entering into our fall season of life. By the time we get to be in the sixties, we can say that we're entering into our winter season, and we have a few days remaining on the earth. In Genesis 6:3, "And the Lord said my spirit shall not always strive with man, for that he also is flesh, yet his days: shall be 120 years," the Bible tells us that a man's days shall be 120 years. If we divide that into four seasons, thirty years of age would be considered spring and from thirty to sixty years of age would be summer and from sixty to ninety would be fall and from ninety to 120 years of age would be winter.

In the springtime, everything begins to form bulbs. You can see the trees, the flowers, and the grass begin to grow, and we can see that winter has passed and a new season has begun.

In the summer, we see leaves have formed in the trees, and everything is so green. The birds have begun to build their nest. The gardens are being planted. Animals are giving birth to their young. The birds are singing in the morning, and everything is warm and cozy. And this would be considered the summer season of life.

In the fall, we see the change in the leaves, and everything begins to turn a different color. When we see this, we begin to see the leaf withering and beginning to die. People also have a fall season of life. In the fall season of their lives, men and women likewise begin to see their bodies beginning to change, and we can tell that we are in our fall season of life because of the changes in our bodies. Our hair color changes. We can see the signs of aging all around us in our mortal bodies.

In the season of winter, if we look at nature, we see the trees are bare, and there is no life. Everything seems to be dry and withered; leaves now have fallen to the ground. They are brittle. Mankind also has his winter season. We become brittle, and when we look into the mirror, we can see that we are aging. We find that we can't do the things that we used to be able to do. Then we see that we are as the trees, and our time is near that we too wither and die.

Truly, there are four seasons in this life—spring, summer, fall, and winter. This is in the natural man or in nature.

There is also a spring or a new birth on the spiritual side of life. It is when we believe in our hearts that God has raised Jesus from the dead and we have asked Jesus to come into our hearts and to forgive us of our sins. At that time, we are just like the baby born in the natural man. We are born again through the spiritual man and have eternal life through Christ Jesus, our Lord. And with this, we are promised eternal life. *This is truly the fountain of youth—being born of God!*

> For God so loved the world, that he gave his only begotten Son, that whosoever believes in him should not perish but have everlasting life. (John 3:16)

We have a newness of life, and because of our faith in Jesus Christ, we have eternal life through him, and we will never die.

Those born again in the Lord will never die. They will never grow old, and they will live forever.

Every answer to life's problems is found in the book below—the Holy Bible!

Chapter 12

Faith in the Supernatural God

Let us look at what faith is. What is faith? And what does faith consist of?

When one is going through a major sickness or disease in his life, one begins to realize that all our hope does not revolve around medical science or medical wisdom of the doctors. We can go to the doctor when we have a major illness or sickness only to discover that the doctor is limited only to the knowledge that he has regarding the treatments for the sickness or disease that a person has.

Medical treatments one would receive during his illness or disease are based on a doctor's expertise and knowledge gained from his education. When a person's sickness or illness supersedes a doctor's training, then that doctor will do a referral to another doctor, whose training and expertise supersede those of the former. The more knowledge that a doctor has, the better he can treat a sickness or disease. And when he has done everything that he can by his knowledge, he then makes a referral so that someone else can take the treatment for the illness to our higher level.

During a sickness or disease, there comes a time when the sickness becomes untreatable and there is no knowledge of any treatment that will cure or control that sickness or disease. And at that time, we must have an option for knowledge greater than our disease, and that knowledge and belief are based on something that is not controlled by a natural treatment but is treated by a supernatural treatment. And that is when we find faith in a *supernatural god.*

So let us look at what faith is in the supernatural.

Let us look at *Webster's Dictionary*'s definition for *supernatural*:

- The existence or occurring existence or occurring outside the experience and knowledge of man, not explainable by the known forces and laws of nature, involving or attributed to God or a god.

Sometimes our medical treatments and our sicknesses cannot be cured by man. Therefore, we must seek out supernatural help.

Let's look at this time and see about supernatural help and where we can find it.

One way we can find out more about the supernatural help is by looking into the Holy Bible and what it says about faith.

Now faith is the substance of things hoped for the evidence of things not seen. (Hebrews 11:1)

For by it the elders obtained a good report. (Hebrews 11:2)

Through faith we understand that the worlds were framed by the word of God so that the things which are seen were not made of things which do appear. (Hebrews 11:3)

By faith Abel offered unto God a more excellent sacrifice than Cain, by which he obtained witness that he was righteous, God testifying of his gifts and by it he being dead yet, speaks. (Hebrews 11:4)

By faith Enoch was translated that he should not see death; and was not found, because God had translated him: for before his translation he had this testimony that he pleased God. (Hebrews 11:5)

So we found out what supernatural faith is!

Faith is the substance of things hoped for and the evidence of things not yet seen.

So faith says "Even though I am sick, I know that I will become well." So when the doctor tells us he has done everything that he can or maybe even says "You will have to live with this sickness for the rest of your life," we can have faith in a supernatural god, that when man has done all that he can with our treatments, at that time, we can say, "I have faith in God!"

Is any sick among you? Let him call for the elders of the church and let them pray over him (anointing) him with oil in the name of the Lord. (James 5:14)

And the prayer of faith shall save the sick and the Lord shall
raise him up and if he had committed sins, they shall be forgiven
him. (James 5:15)

Confess your faults one to another, and pray one for another, that
ye may be healed. The effectual fervent prayer of a righteous man
availeth much. (James 5:16)

Just like when we have to go to the doctor for illnesses and when he has
done all that he can for us during our sickness, he, at that time, would do a
referral to another doctor, who has a greater knowledge of the treatment for
our illness. We, likewise, must seek out those who have faith
in a supernatural god and believe his words that we
may be able to receive the promises of that god and
what that god has said—that we can have anything
that he has spoken unto us through faith in his Word.
We see in the Word of God that there is healing!

If the local church that we are attending does not have faith in healing
or does not practice those things that are biblical pertaining to healing,
then we can never receive our healing there because of their unbelief on
what scripture says. So we must find a church that practices faith in the
scriptures pertaining to anointing the sick with oil as scripture has indicated
for all those who are going through a sickness or a disease so that we can
see an answer to prayer and a manifestation of the supernatural power of
God.

In every full gospel-based church, they should call for the elders of the
church and have them anoint the sick with oil and pray for them, that by

faith, God would heal the sick, and if they have committed any sins, they shall be forgiven.

Faith comes into our hearts when we believe God's Word is true and we act upon what it says, and when we do that which God has said, we can, at that time, receive by faith every promise of God's Word. When can God move for us? It is when we believe from our hearts that his Word is true. At that time, God can move for us and grant us the things that we need in this life until the time that we leave this world, and even in death. Jesus proclaimed, "I will never leave you. I will never forsake you; I will go with you. Even unto the end of the world."

We must look into God's promises and hold on to them and obey them, and by acting upon what it says, we can receive his promises for his Word is supernatural. And in the event that we are not seeing his supernatural power or his promises, then it is at that time that we should ask God for his referral to a church home that practices the things of God. By attending a church that has faith in biblical principles, we will find out all his promises for us in this life—that when we leave this world, we can have a place for our eternal rest, which is called heaven, where we will live and never grow old and where we will never die—and we will live forever in accordance to the Word of God and through faith in God, and in him we have eternal life through Jesus Christ, our Lord.

During every sickness, you will find yourself seeking knowledge not only from the doctors, and in my case, I was always looking for divine intervention even though my health was improving. I had an episode of an unexpected sickness called gout. During this sickness, I was on crutches. And it was not fun being on crutches. My wife prayed for me on a couple of occasions. I called for the elders of the church, and our pastors prayed over me and anointed me with oil. I did not receive the manifestation of my healing even though I had obeyed the Word of God and did what the scriptures had said for me to do.

I began to examine my life and see if there was anywhere that I had disobeyed the spirit of the Lord that could possibly cause or allow Satan to attack my body with sickness. There was one instance in particular when I had not obeyed the spirit of the Lord. This was where the Lord laid it upon my heart to give my mother-in-law a TV. So I decided that what I would do is take the TV to my mother-in-law even if I did not have any help. I was going get the TV to my mother-in-law as soon as possible. So I went downstairs to get the two-wheel dolly in order to place the TV on it. I moved the television from our house, loaded it on my pickup truck, and drove to my mother-in-law's house to give her the television. Earlier in the year, my mother-in-law had made a statement while we were visiting her house that she would love to have a bigger TV. Her eyesight was failing her, and she wanted to have a bigger TV. This would allow her to have better vision of the program that was on television (this would make everything bigger, and she would be able to see it better). I had been fighting this gout and had been on crutches, and I wanted to find a way to get rid of it; and if I had been disobedient in any way, shape, or form, I wanted to repent of it and make it right with the Lord so that I could receive my healing.

I simply had made up my mind that I was going to obey the Lord.

When I arrived at my mother-in-law's house, she came out and asked what I was doing, and I said, "I am bringing you your TV that you requested." She said, "But you did not have to do that!" My response was "The Lord had laid it upon my heart to bring you this TV, and I want to ask you to forgive me because I should have brought this TV over to you several months ago." She forgave me for not bringing in the TV sooner. I think she was very surprised. In fact, so surprised I do not think she knew what to say. We got everything hooked up for her, and she was enjoying her bigger TV, and she finally said, "I cannot believe this!"

I told her that the Lord had heard her request and that he had laid it upon my heart to bring her the television and that I had I wanted to make things right with the Lord in any area where I had not been obedient. This would make a way for me to be able to receive my healing, and I would have nothing blocking the way.

> *For rebellion is as the sin of witchcraft and 'stubbornness is as iniquity and idolatry. Because thou hast rejected the word of the Lord, He (hast) (has) also rejected ('the) (you) from being King. (1 Samuel 15:23)

> And Saul said unto Samuel, I have sinned: for I have transgressed the commandment of the Lord and thy words: because I feared the people and obeyed their voice. (1 Samuel 15:24)

Saul was in trouble for disobedience. We find here in the scripture that rebellion was just like the sin of witchcraft. I wanted to make sure that I had not been disobedient to God in any form or fashion, and I wanted to make things right with the Lord so nothing would be there to block my healing.

So I went to the doctor, and the doctor wrote me a prescription, but this prescription did not help me any. So the doctor wrote me another prescription, and my condition improved a little, but there was still a lot of discomfort. So we made an appointment and went back to the physician. And this time, it was with my family physician, and she prescribed me an injection plus gave me a new medication that may improve the symptoms of the gout.

So after the injection, I began to feel somewhat better, but then the next day, I noticed that there was still a great discomfort and increase of pain, so I told my wife to stop and get the prescription filled. When she got home, I looked at the prescription and became very disappointed. I had looked at all the side effects that this new medication had and actually became very angry due to the fact that medical science is putting medicines in the market with side effects that could possibly make me develop a sickness or disease that would be a greater illness than the gout that I already had. A lot of the new medications that are on the market today do have a lot of side effects that can cause a person to have an illness greater than the sickness or disease he has at the current time.

After seeing the side effects, and I quote from the warning label: *"may rarely cause a certain or serious, even fatal muscle damage and lead to serious kidney problem."

Let us look at *Webster's Dictionary* for the definition of *heart*: *"the hollow, muscular organ in a vertebrate animal that receives blood from the brain and pumps it through the arteries by alternative dilation and contraction."

After seeing this label, it simply made me angry—it made me so angry, in fact, I wanted to threw the medicine down, and the top came off and majority of the pills poured out of the bottle. I simply could not believe that our modern-day medicines could kill someone while trying to improve their health, illness, or disease!

Just take a look at most modern-day commercials that are on television and just take in consideration all the side effects that come on the TV advertisements. A lot of them tell you to check your liver constantly as the side effects could cause liver damage among other things. Some new medications cause you to have kidney problems. Some cause cancer, and many other medical illnesses can develop in someone who is using the modern-day medicines.

So when I saw all the side effects from all the medications that I had purchased, I simply became very angry, as I have stated in this book.

My wife told me that I needed to take the medication in order to get better, that the gout could spread to other parts of my body, and that I would need to take my medication.

I did, in fact, take one pill before I went to bed, and I woke up the next morning after having a dream. I felt like the dream was possibly a warning from the Lord. My wife left for work that day, around 6:10 a.m. I began to talk to the Lord in prayer. And while talking to the Lord in prayer, I remembered then that my wife had purchased me some olive oil at the grocery store on the same night that she picked up my prescriptions.

Olive oil is used in a lot of churches—when the pastor calls for the elders of the church and the pastor and elders take the olive oil and anoint the sick, and they pray over him the prayer of faith that God would heal him and deliver him from his sickness or disease. So it came to me—I believe by the spirit of the Lord—to go into the kitchen, get a tablespoon, find the olive oil, open it up, pour out two tablespoons of olive oil, drink it, and pray and ask the Lord, saying, "Lord, this is your olive oil. Lord, when I take this olive oil, let this oil go to the joints of my toes and bring healing to me in mighty name of Jesus." And at that time, faith came alive in my heart, and I believed that I could receive the promises of the Lord and receive my healing.

"Now Faith is the substance of things hoped for, and the evidence of things not yet seen," says Hebrews 11:1.

I am glad that I have come to the knowledge that there is a supernatural god. And when all else fails, I can trust in the one who created the world by his spoken word.

> And God said let there be light: and there was light. (Genesis 1:3)

> And God saw the light, that it was good: and God divided the light from the darkness. (Genesis 1:4)

> And God called the light Day, and the darkness he called Night. And the evening and the morning were the first Day. (Genesis 1:5)

To think about having a relationship with a supernatural god and that you have fellowship with that god, and with the relationship with God, you could call upon Jesus when there is no other hope, that is when your faith comes alive. And from your heart, you cry out to the supernatural god, asking him to intervene in your situation, in your trials, or in your troubles, and God would hear you when you pray and will answer your prayer. Thank God for that relationship that you can have with that supernatural god.

Within twenty-four hours, I began to notice that there was a great improvement in my gout condition. It always pays to try and to be obedient to the spirit of the Lord and to move and to do what God has asked you to do. Because we're not living in a perfect world, there will always be illnesses and difficulties in the human life that one must go through and face on a daily basis.

Chapter 13

Allowing the Supernatural God to Become Lord of Your Life

You may be asking the question, "How do I find faith in the supernatural god?"

There is nothing greater in life than to know that you have made peace with a supernatural god, and everything that you have ever done in this life that was wrong is totally forgiven. And you know in your heart that God has forgiven you of all your past sins and transgressions, and you are walking in the newness of that which God has given you.

You may have never asked the supernatural god to become your god, or you may have never asked God to come into your life, or you may not be walking in this life the way you should, in accordance to the Bible. Maybe you have been disobedient and not doing the things that God has asked you to do. So I want to lead you in a simple prayer at this time, whether you've been disobedient or if you have not walked in full obedience to the Word of God. At this time, if you would read this prayer with me, I believe God will hear this prayer and God will come into your life, and he will become your Lord and your savior.

My prayer for you:

Lord, I believe you are a supernatural god. You are the only god that has risen from the dead. I ask you, God, to forgive me of my sins. I ask you to come into my heart, come into my life, change my heart, and change my life. I believe that you rose from the dead and that you are sitting at the right hand of God. And today, because I have asked you to forgive me of my sins, to come into my heart, to change my heart, and to change my life, I believe that right now I am passed from death to life. Right now I am saved. Right now I am delivered. Amen. Thank you, Lord.

Chapter 14

Living in the Moment and Day to Day

There had been many times in my life during my recent sickness that my wife and I had to live in the moment and day to day.

My wife and I have found that we must rely on, trust in, and believe in supernatural intervention during these times of decision that we must have and believe in God's supernatural help to live in the moment and day to day.

Our prayer life is very important during the time of sickness and disease. It is a very important part of life. We must make every decision based upon the Word of God. We must be led by the spirit of God in order to be successful during this time of illness.

*But they that wait upon the Lord shall renew their strength they
shall mount up wings as eagles, they shall run and not be weary;
and they shall walk and not faint. (Isaiah 40:31)

It is very important for all of us in the time of sickness and disease or in the time of trouble to be willing to say, "I cannot receive my health in any other way than through the Word of God." And at that time, we begin to live in the moment and live day to day by putting our trust and confidence in the things that God has said through his Word, spending time in prayer, seeking the will of God, and asking God, "What should I do?"

Making every decision during that sickness or that disease or in that time of trouble, looking into what the Word of God says pertaining to our situation, and then acting upon what the Word of God has said and receiving them by faith, then we can say at that time that we are living in the moment and day to day.

*MANY ARE THE AFFLICTIONS OF THE RIGHTEOUS: BUT THE LORD DELIVERED HIM OUT OF THEM ALL. (Psalm 34:19)

The Bible clearly tells us that many are the afflictions of the righteous, but the Lord delivered him out of them all.

In every problem, in every situation, God reveals himself to those who are in trouble—those that believe, trust, and call upon his name. There is always hope through Jesus Christ, our Lord.

There are many people in the Bible who have faced death, who have been beaten, who have been placed in jail, and who have been crucified. All these things we find in the Bible. These people found faith in God, and God moved in their lives and delivered them and set them free no matter what they were facing; and even being crucified in death, they rose again and had eternal life because God has raised Jesus from the dead.

We should be very thankful that we have another day to live. When we get up in the morning and we open our eyes, we should say each day,

"Thank you, Lord, for another day that I can spend time with my family and with my friends, and help me, Lord, to do your will. Today, Lord, help me win another soul for your kingdom that they may come to know you as Lord and Savior and that their needs could also be met through Jesus Christ, our Lord."

The book of Isaiah 54:17 says:

*No weapon that is formed against thee shall prosper, and every tongue that shall rise up against thee in judgment thou (shalt) (shall) condemn. This is the heritage of the servants of the Lord, and their righteousness is of me, saith the Lord.

No matter what we are going through, the book of Isaiah tells us that no weapon formed against us shall prosper and that we will have victory through the Lord Jesus Christ because our righteousness is of him, called Jesus. We can overcome anything that has come against us in this life because Jesus himself overcame, and we have faith in Jesus Christ that our victory is in him and our faith is in him, and we shall overcome all things because Jesus himself overcame all things, even in death. God raised him from the dead, and we of like faith, when the last trump of God shall sound, the dead in Christ shall rise first. And those who are alive and remain shall be changed in a moment in the twinkling of an eye, and so shall they ever be with the Lord. This is the victory of the saints!

Notes

* The Holy Bible, King James Version (Nelson Regency, 1990).

* Carilion Clinic Sleep Center.

* Carilion Family Physicians.

* Carilion: Roanoke Memorial Hospital.

* Carilion Clinic, Westlake.

* *Webster's New World Dictionary*, 3rd college ed. (Simon & Schuster, Inc., 1998). This edition is a major revision of *Webster's New World Dictionary*, second college edition

About the Author

F. D. Williams—an everyday American working hard to make a living for his family. This is his story and how his family came to know about his sleeping disorder.

To contact F. D. Williams:

For a seminar at your local church or a conference, you can notify us by e-mail: saltwillie@hotmail.com.